The Ecosystem of a
Stream

Elaine Pascoe Photography by **Dwight Kuhn**

The Rosen Publishing Group's
PowerKids Press™
New York

Published in 2003 by The Rosen Publishing Group, Inc.
29 East 21st Street, New York, NY 10010

First Edition

Editor: Nancy MacDonell Smith
Book Design: Michael J. Caroleo

Photo Credits: Photos © Dwight Kuhn.

Pascoe, Elaine.
The ecosystem of a stream / Elaine Pascoe.— 1st ed.
    p. cm. — (The library of small ecosystems)
Summary: Simple text describes the plants and animals that inhabit a stream, creating an interrelated ecosystem.
Includes bibliographical references (p.   ).
ISBN 0-8239-6307-1 (lib. bdg.)
1. Stream ecology—Juvenile literature. [1. Stream ecology. 2. Ecology.] I. Title.
QH541.5.S7 P37 2003
577.6'4—dc21

                              2001007786

Manufactured in the United States of America

Contents

The Stream

A stream flows through a forest. Its clear water rushes over rocks and swirls into deep pools. The water looks empty, but it is not. A stream is home to many plants and animals. Many more live along its banks.

The plants, the animals, and the stream itself are all part of a small ecosystem, a community of living and nonliving things. Fish, insects, birds, and other living things that are part of this community depend on the stream and one another to **survive**. Every part of the ecosystem has a role to play. Even the sunlight that filters through the trees is important.

Everything from the trees growing above the stream to the fish that swim in the stream's waters is part of this small ecosystem.

5

In the Water

Fish and many other kinds of animals live in the stream. Just as you breathe air, these animals breathe oxygen that is in the water, through organs called **gills**. The stream is the animals' home and their source of food.

The crayfish lives in streams but it is not a fish, despite its name. It is a **crustacean**. It has a hard outer coat that protects its soft body. Its front legs have **pincers** for grasping its food. Crayfish will eat almost anything, but they mostly eat plants that grow in the water.

A female crayfish lays eggs, which she carries on the underside of her body for about six months. The eggs hatch in the spring. The baby crayfish stay with their mother for a short time before swimming off on their own.

The brook trout is one kind of fish that lives in a stream.

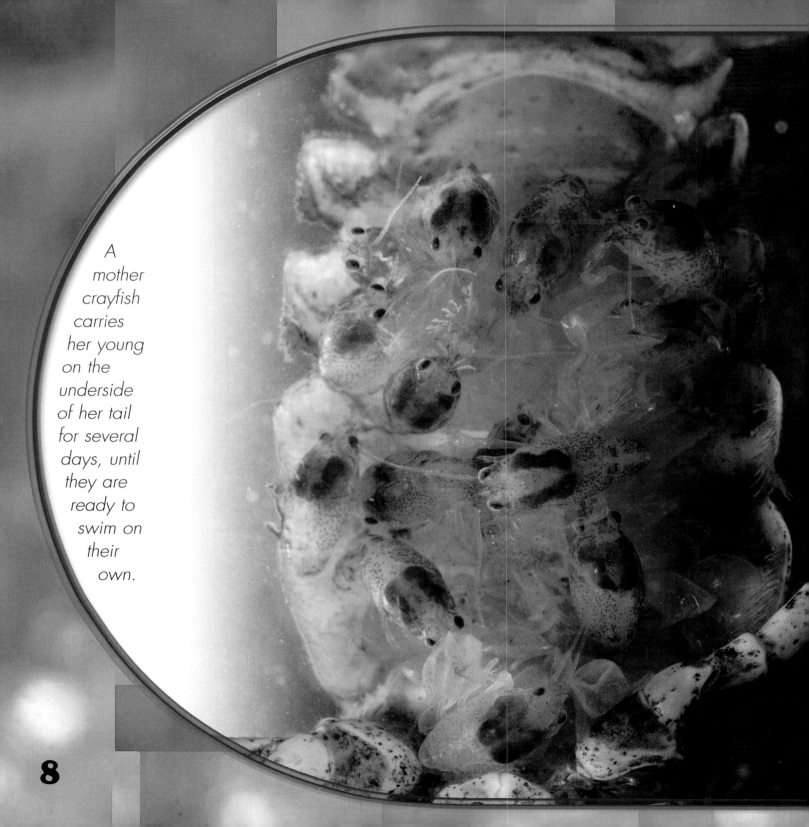

A mother crayfish carries her young on the underside of her tail for several days, until they are ready to swim on their own.

8

Despite its name, the crayfish is not a fish. It belongs to a group of animals called crustaceans. The crayfish's hard shell helps to protect it from animals that might want to eat it.

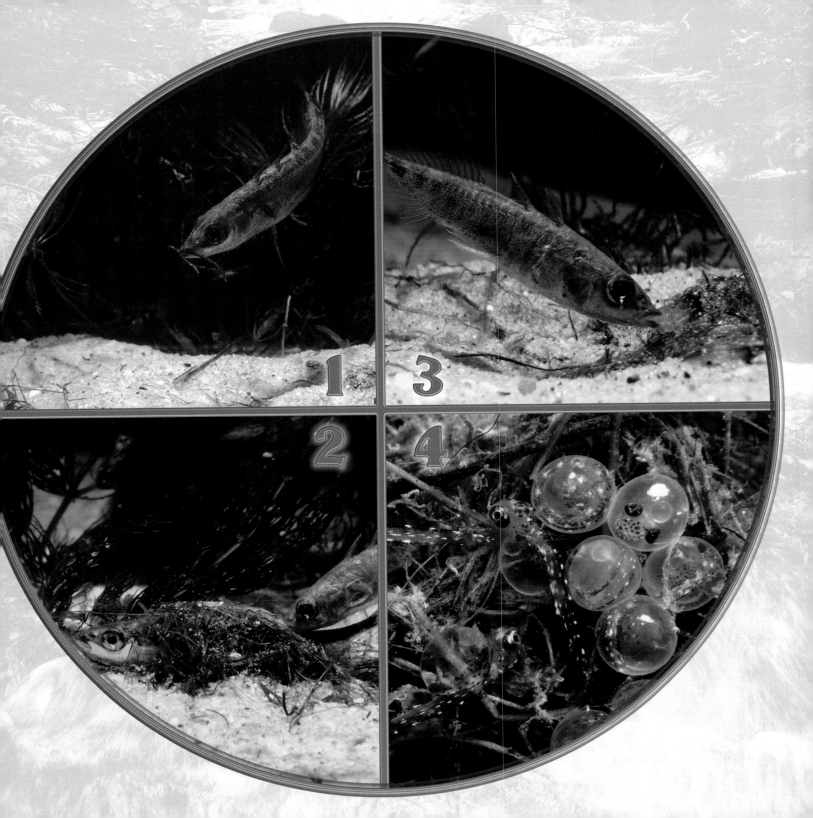

A Fish's Nest

Sticklebacks also raise their young in the stream. Sticklebacks are small fish named for the sharp spines on their backs. Few fish work harder than do sticklebacks at raising their young. It is the male stickleback that does most of the work.

At breeding time, the male stickleback builds a nest from bits of plants. He finds a female and herds her to the nest. The male pokes the female's tail to encourage her to lay eggs, and then he **fertilizes** the eggs.

The male stays at the nest, fanning the eggs with his fins to keep water moving over them. The eggs hatch in about six days.

1: *The male stickleback carries pieces of plants with which to build a nest.* 2: *The male pokes the female so she'll lay her eggs.* 3: *Stickleback eggs look like clear balls.* 4: *The stickleback young remain in the nest for a few days after they hatch.*

A Double Life

Frogs, newts, and salamanders begin their lives in the stream. As adults, they live on land, often on the banks of the stream. These animals are called **amphibians**. That name comes from Greek words that mean "double life."

Young amphibians hatch from eggs that their mothers lay in water. The newly hatched young look like little fish. They breathe water through gills. They change slowly. They grow legs, which allow them to walk. They grow lungs, which allow them to breathe air. These changes take either weeks or months, depending on the kind of animal. When the changes are complete, the animals leave the water for a life on land.

Top: *Red-spotted newts are red as babies but brown as adults. Adult newts live in the water.* Bottom: *Newts live in the water for the first month of their lives. Then they leave the water and spend from two to three years on land.*

The leopard frog gets its name from its dark spots, which look like the spots of a leopard. These spots protect the leopard frog from its enemies by helping it blend in with its surroundings.

14

Two-lined salamanders can sometimes be found among moss or under rocks at the edge of a stream.

Small Swimmers

Animals such as fish and frogs are easy to see. You must look closely to find other creatures that live in the water. Tiny flatworms are just ½ inch (1.3 cm) long. Water fleas are so small that you need a microscope to see them. Small animals such as these are often eaten by larger animals.

The young, or **larvae**, of some insects live in the water, too. One of these is the caddisfly. A caddisfly larva builds its own tube-shaped case, using tiny sticks and other materials it finds. It binds these materials together with silk that its body makes. The caddisfly drags its case along as it crawls around the bottom of the stream.

Top: *The water flea carries its young in a pouch until they're ready to live on their own.* Bottom: *A caddisfly larva covers itself with a case made of tiny sticks and other materials.*

From Water to Air

A stream is a nursery for insects called dragonflies, too. A young dragonfly is called a **nymph**. Nymphs hatch from eggs that females lay in the water. They look a lot like adults, but they have no wings.

A dragonfly nymph may live in the stream for several years. As it grows, it will **molt**, or shed its skin, ten or more times. Finally it is ready to leave the water. It crawls up a plant or a rock and molts again. When the insect leaves its old skin this time, it has wings. It is an adult.

Dragonflies are **predators**. The nymphs and adults both catch and eat insects that live in or near the stream.

Top right: *The dragonfly nymph lives in the stream for several years.*
Center left: *Eventually the dragonfly will grow wings and shed its skin.*
Bottom right: *Adult dragonflies live near the stream and hunt for insects.*

Adult
mayflies
do not eat.
Some live only
for a day, just long
enough to mate and
to lay eggs.

A mayfly enters the next
stage of its life. It leaves
the water, sheds its
skin, and flies
away.

This flatworm is shown more than four times its actual size. In real life, flatworms are only ½ inch (1.3 cm) long.

Mayfly young also live in streams. They feed on plant material.

The water strider can skate over the surface of the water on its long legs. These insects are often found in streams.

21

Along the Banks

A stream is a source of water, which all living things need. Many animals come to the banks to drink. A shy meadow **vole** sips from the **shallow** water at the edge of the stream. A coyote steps right into the water and takes a drink.

Marsh marigolds and other plants grow along the damp banks of the stream. They soak up water through their roots. The stream helps the plants in another way, too. As it cuts through the forest, the stream makes an opening in the trees. Sunlight pours down. The plants use the energy in sunlight to make their own food. They turn water and carbon dioxide, a gas in the air, into a kind of sugar.

A stream lets light and air into the forest. This helps plants and trees to grow. Inset: For animals such as this coyote, a stream is a source of drinking water.

Birds at the Stream

A stream is a fine place for a mother mallard duck to raise a brood of chicks. Ducks, such as the mallard, eat plants, seeds, insects, and other things that they find in the water and along the banks. Some of the other birds that live along the stream are hunters. Long-legged blue herons wade in the water at the edge of the stream, hoping to catch fish and frogs with their beaks.

The kingfisher is a daring hunter. It dives headfirst into the stream to catch a fish. The bird carries its meal to a branch nearby and swallows it whole.

A mother mallard duck and her young swim in the stream. The chicks follow their mother closely wherever she goes.

The great blue heron wades through shallow water at the edge of the stream, hunting for small fish and other things to eat.

The kingfisher comes to the stream to hunt. It dives into the water to catch its food.

The meadow vole doesn't go out into the deep waters of the stream. It drinks from pools near the edges of the stream.

The kingfisher carries its food to a nearby branch and eats it there.

More Hunters at the Stream

A stream is a good hunting ground for many animals. The water shrew is small, but it is a fierce predator. It swims underwater to catch a frog that is nearly as big as itself!

Raccoons hunt for food in the shallows and along the banks of the stream. A raccoon uses its front paws to turn over rocks and feel around on the stream's floor. When the raccoon catches a crayfish or other **prey**, it handles the prey with its paws before eating it. The raccoon seems to be washing its food, but it is really just turning the prey this way and that.

Top: *A water shrew pulls a frog it has caught out of the stream.*
Bottom: *Raccoons have strong claws that they use to feel for prey in the stream.*

The Stream Community

A stream is a home for water animals and a nursery for young insects. It provides water and helps bring sunlight to plants. The living things in and around the stream depend on the stream, and they depend on one another. The plants provide food for insects and other animals. Some of the plant eaters become food for predators. Predators keep the number of plant eaters from growing too large, so the plants are not all eaten.

Living things everywhere depend on others in much the same way. The stream is just one of Earth's many small ecosystems.

Glossary

amphibians (am-FIH-bee-unz) A group of animals that spend the first part of their lives in water and the rest on land.

crustacean (krus-TAY-shun) An animal with a hard outer coat, a body divided into sections, and many jointed legs.

fertilizes (FUR-tih-lyz-iz) Introduces male reproductive cells into the female to begin development.

gills (GILZ) Body parts for taking oxygen from water, or breathing water.

larvae (LAHR-vee) The plural form of larva; the early life stage of certain animals that differs greatly from the adult stage.

molt (MOHLT) To shed skin or any outer covering.

nymph (NIMF) The young of certain insects.

pincers (PINT-surz) Sharp claws on a crustacean.

predators (PREH-duh-terz) An animal that catches and eats other animals.

prey (PRAY) An animal that is caught and eaten by another animal.

shallow (SHA-loh) Not deep.

survive (sur-VYV) To stay alive.

vole (VOHL) A small animal that is a member of the mouse family.

Index

Web Sites

Due to the changing nature of Internet links, PowerKids Press has developed an online list of Web sites related to the topic of this book. This site is updated regularly. Please use this link to access the list:
www.powerkidslinks.com/lse/streameco/